Contents

Written by	Gerry Bailey
Publisher	Felicia Law
Managing Editors	Joanna Buck & Sam Sweeney
Design Director	Simon Webb
Designers	Claire Penny & Simon Oon
Creative Director	Tracy Carrington
Editor	Dawn Sirett
Illustrations	Creative Design of Advocate & Henryk Jansor
Production Manager	Victoria Grimsell
Production Controller	Christina Schuster

Mars Images pages 68-71 courtesy of NASA

Based on the TV series 'Butt-Ugly Martians'
© 2000 Just Entertainment Ltd/Mike Young Productions Inc

This publication is conceived, edited and designed by Just Editions Ltd (an imprint of Marshall Editions Ltd – a wholly-owned subsidiary of The Just Group plc)

Published by Just Editions Ltd
74, Shepherd's Bush Green
London W12 8QE

Printed and bound by Proost Groupe CPI, Belgium

ISBN 1903912 27 X

Catch them on the web: www.buttuglymartians.com / www.stoatmuldoon.com

BUTT-UGLY MARTIANS™

ANNUAL 2002

Written by Gerry Bailey

BUTT-UGLY BOUNTY

TODAY'S A SPECIAL DAY FOR THE BUTT-UGLY MARTIANS!

I CAN'T BELIEVE IT'S BEEN A YEAR ALREADY..

BELIEVE IT BABE. WE MUST HAVE DEFENDED THIS PLANET A HUNDRED TIMES.

IT'S HUNGRY WORK.

AND I'VE GOT THE BUTT-UGLY BRUISES TO PROVE IT.

IT'S THE ONE-YEAR ANNIVERSARY OF THE MARTIANS COMING TO EARTH, AND A PARTY IS CALLED FOR ...

HOW DID YOU MANAGE TO TRICK EMPEROR BOG?

HEY, KEEP HIM SUPPLIED WITH PHONY REPORTS AND HE'S A HAPPY EMPEROR.

HE STILL THINKS YOU'RE REALLY CONQUERING EARTH.

MY BLOATWORM NACHOS ARE READY!

DING

LITTLE HELP HERE, FELLAS.

I JUST SENT HIM OUR LATEST PHONY VICTORY COMPLETE WITH QUINTOPHONIC SOUND AND 3-D GLASSES.

OOPS!

AHH. BURNT TO A CRISP. JUST THE WAY I LIKE 'EM.

WE FAKED INVADING...

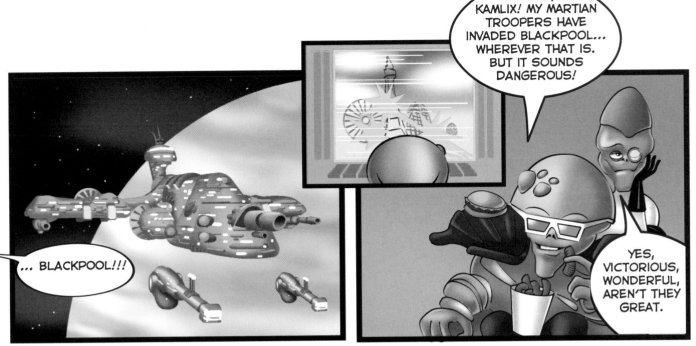

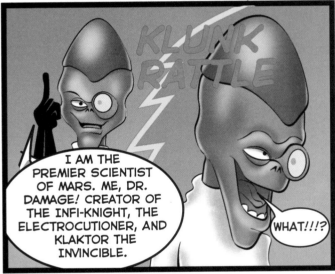

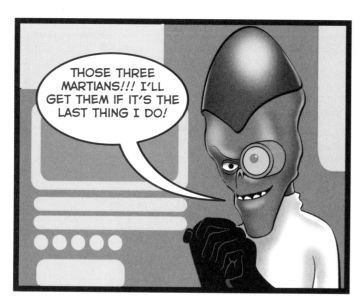

THOSE THREE MARTIANS!!! I'LL GET THEM IF IT'S THE LAST THING I DO!

IT'S BEEN A YEAR NOW...

... SINCE EVIL ALIEN SCUM ACTIVITY ON EARTH HAS SKYROCKETED TO GARGANTUAN LEVELS.

SO I THINK I DESERVE ONE DAY OFF, DON'T YOU, RONALD?

BUT WHO WILL DEFEND THE PLANET? WHO WILL SAVE THE EARTH FROM EVIL EXTRATERRESTRIALS?

I WILL... I'LL JUST DO IT TOMORROW. AHH... NOW THAT'S A GREAT CUPPA!

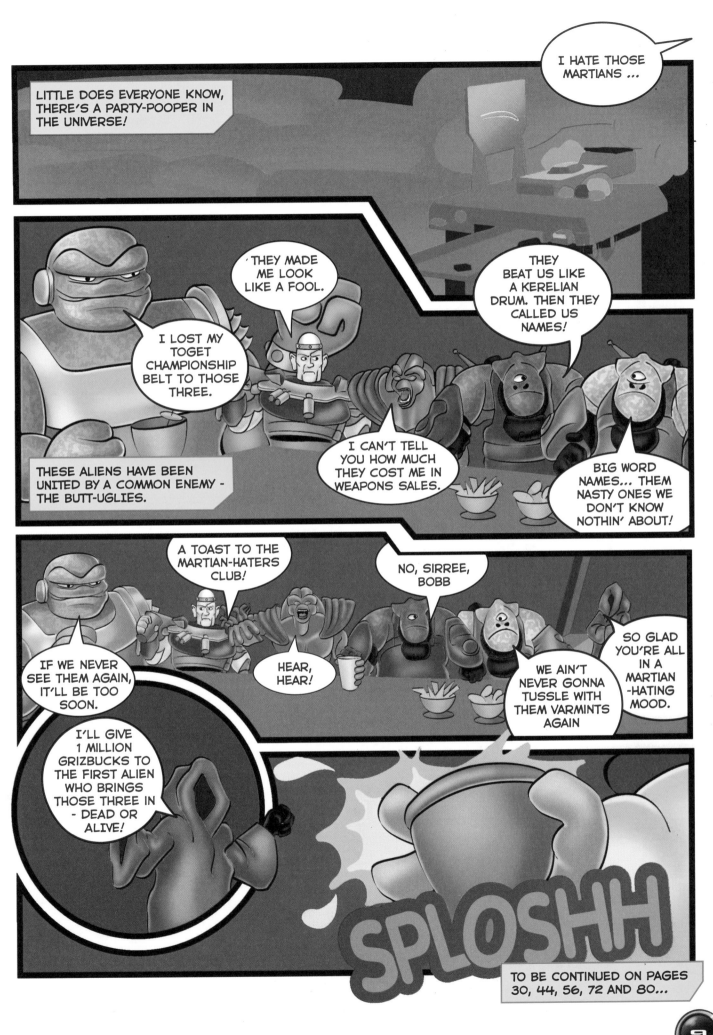

TO BE CONTINUED ON PAGES 30, 44, 56, 72 AND 80...

FUTURE PUZZLES

"Stoat Muldoon here, folks. Roll-up for the ride of a lifetime. Join me on an awesome alien tracking expedition. But first, I'll have to check if you're made of the right stuff to take on this dangerous, death-defying mission."

PUZZLE 1

Let's start by making sure that you know exactly what's what and who's who. Solve this riddle to discover the name of Public Enemy Number One

My first is in mat, but not seen in fat.

My second's in flag and also in bat.

My third is in reel and you'll see it in road.

My fourth is in tiger and also in toad.

My fifth is in ink, but never in bank.

My sixth is in apple and also in tank.

My seventh is last - it's in new and in net

It's also in nice, but it's not seen in jet.

DOWNLOADING 85%

Write your answer here

10

PUZZLE 2

Are your eyes sharp enough for this job? Take a close look at this satellite photograph of a disused warehouse. My super-sensitive MATD (Muldoon's Alien Tracking Device) has picked up the presence of huge numbers of aliens hiding out in this area. Can you count how many are lying in wait for us?

Write your answer here

PUZZLE 3

We'll be breaking the barriers of science and technology on our epic journey, so we'll need to be super-smart. Do you think you're up to the challenge? Let's see if you can open this locked box I found in an alien's hideout. The numbers seem to have fallen off the keypad on the lock. Can you put them back in the right places and get the box open?

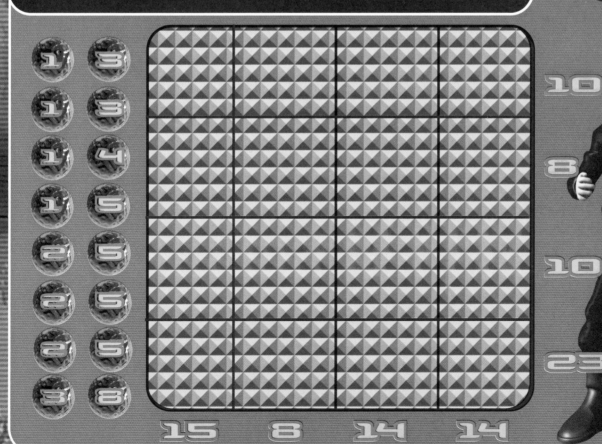

Hot tip: Each row and column must add up to the numbers on the side and bottom.

Emperor Bog

With his evil sights set on conquering Earth, the tyrannical Emperor Bog spends his days happily tormenting Earthlings and aliens alike!

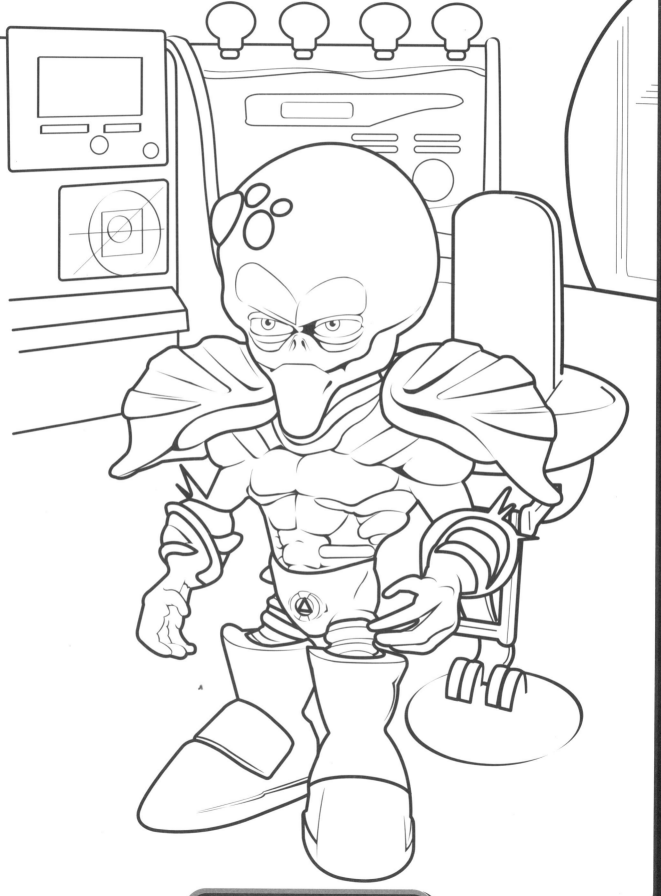

COLOUR IN

Dr. Damage

Dr Damage is the Emperor Bog's loyal henchman. But in truth, the ruthless alien scientist has a sinister plan for world domination of his own...

COLOUR IN

WEBSITES
THE INVASION HITS THE INTERNET

Visited www.buttuglymartians.com yet? The site's just crammed with brilliant features! You can expand your Martian knowledge, send digi-cards to your friends and collect valuable Martian Points!

RETINA SCANNER

MOTION PLAYER

FILE SEARCH

WWW.BUTTUGLYMARTIANS.COM

PLAY GAMES!

MATCH THE MARTIANS WHILE WAITING FOR OUR SITE TO LOAD!

Drag the planet Mars to the correct definition of the Martian term.
Click the VIEW DATABASE button to see how many you've gotten right!

TERM# 1

BLOATWORMS

- A slimy, gooey Martian snack that tastes like chicken
- Fishing bait
- A Martian stomach ache
- Inhabitants of the planet Bloat

DRAG IT TO THE RIGHT ANSWER

VIEW DATABASE

25 left

SUBMIT ▶

A GREKIAN VIRUS RECENTLY CORRUPTED OUR MARTIAN TERMINOLOGY DATABASE. I COULD SURE USE YOUR HELP REBUILDING IT.

MARTIAN TERMINOLOGY DATABASE

Test your Martian knowledge with the Martian Terminology Database! Drag the planet Mars to the correct definition of a Martian term or phrase. Win 50 Martian points for every correct answer!

1   2   3

RECIPIENT'S NAME: RECIPIENT'S EMAIL:

YOUR FIRST NAME: YOUR EMAIL:

MESSAGE:

MARTIAN POINTS

GIBBERIZE ▶

HEY GUYS, MIKE HERE. WANNA DO SOMETHING REALLY COOL? HOW ABOUT SENDING ALL YOUR FRIENDS MESSAGES IN MARTIAN GIBBERISH!

GIBBERISH DECODING STATION

Always being told you speak gibberish? Well, prove people right by sending them a digi-card in Martian Gibberish! Select a card, write a message in Martian Gibberish and then e-mail a friend! When they receive the card they'll be able to run a special translation to read your secret message!

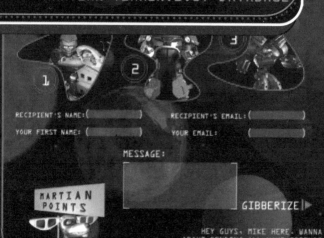

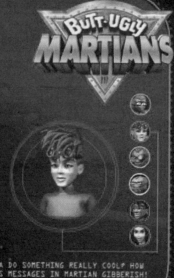

DOWNLOADING

"Greetings Martian warriors. Your mission is taking so long that our mighty Emperor has asked me to check if your brains are still fully operational, or if they've turned into disgusting Earthling JELLY! Can you fill in this crossword and match each letter of the alphabet to a number?"

Emperor Bog realises that your tiny minds are too feeble to crack this cunning puzzle on your own. So he has ordered me to get you started and fill in the bottom line for you sad Martian misfits.

1	2	3	4	5	6	7	8	9	10	11	12	13	14	15	16	17	18	19	20	21	22	23	24	25	26
M	A	R	S						G				O		D										

DOWNLOADING

PUZZLE 2

Here's another brain-jerker to test how well your little green cells are functioning. Make one mistake and you'll be back on the Bogstar and helping me with some VERY interesting experiments I've got going in my lab.

Find the letters that appear only once, and work out what they spell.

Bogstar

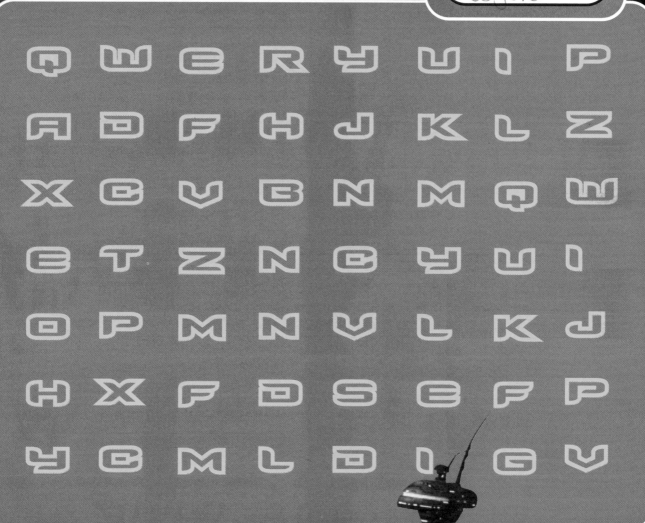

Q W E R Y U I P
A D F H J K L Z
X C V B N M Q W
E T Z N C Y U I
O P M N V L K J
H X F D S E F P
Y C M L D I G V

Q Bog: "Damage, I get a stabbing pain in my eye every time I try to drink this Earth tea."

A Dr. Damage: "Have you tried taking the spoon out of the tea cup, my liege?"

Knock, knock!
Who's there?
Doctor.
Doctor who?
No idiot, Dr. Damage

Teacher:
"If I cut an apple into four pieces, a banana into eight pieces and a cherry into two pieces what do I have?"
Angela: "Fruit salad!"

Q Who won the Miss Beautiful Martian competition last year?

A No-one

Q How do you know when Humanga's under your bed?

A Your nose is pressed against the ceiling!

Q Heard about the alien who was fed up with having just one hand?

A Yeah, he went to the second hand shop to get another one.

DOWNLOADING 85%

PIN.UP

BUTT-UGLY MARTIANS™

B-BOP-A-LUNA

B-T-FRU-T

DO-WAH DIDDI

PIN·UP

BUT·UGLY MARTIANS™

2·T·FRU·T

B·BOP·A·LUNA

DO·WAH DIDDY

The Bogstar v Doomjax

The Bogstar is the mighty battle cruiser that heads Emperor Bog's armada. One of Dr Damage's most impressive creations, it is designed to withstand enemy attack using photon cannons, laser weapons, quaser bombs and planet destroyers.

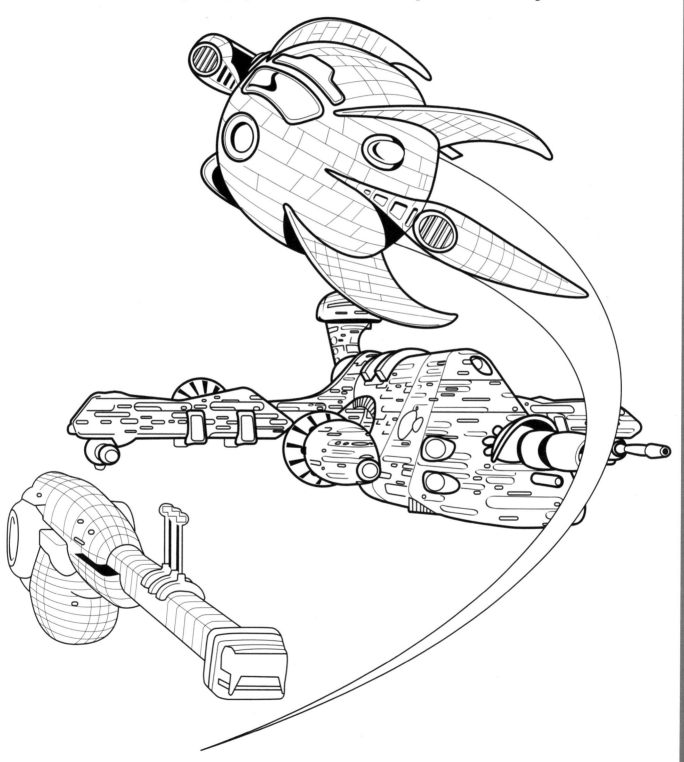

MIKE

In the year 2053, guys like nothing better than to hang out, ride their hoverboards, watch TV or eat burgers (or any other junk food for that matter) and Mike is no exception. Sometimes he's a bit of a hothead, and he can be prone to impetuous behaviour. But he's fiercely loyal to his friends and has no trouble distinguishing right from wrong – wrong being mostly what adults do!

▶▶ Mike likes people and gets on well with everyone, which is a good thing considering who his new friends are. His home is a typical house of the future full of high-tech gizmos, including internet and TV with more channels than you could ever want. There are lots of pay-per-view channels as well, which is good for Mike, who likes to sit around with his friends watching sport, such as the world hoverboard championships.

▶▶ Mike is a master hoverboarder and can beat just about anyone, whether it's racing or stunting. Even a 720^0 sharkwhaker is easy for him to do! In fact, the Hoverboard Park was Mike's second home until they came along – they being the Martians, of course.

▶▶ When he's not at home or on his hoverboard, Quantum Burger's is the place you'll find Mike. It's got the best burgers and fries in the known world.

▶▶ Meeting the Martians was a life-changing experience for Mike. In less time than it takes to pull a 540^0 corkscrew, Mike changed from a typical teenager into a saviour of the world.

Mike's board

ZAPZ

▶▶ These days, it seems, Mike spends more time at ZAPZ, the old games arcade, than at home. He loves to operate the old arcade games that the Butt-Uglies have brought to life again. Unfortunately his competitive spirit sometimes gets the better of him and he will do anything to stop Angela or Cedric beating his Doomrace 2000 score.

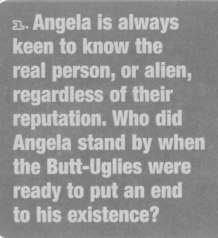

1. Angela is always keen to know the real person, or alien, regardless of their reputation. Who did Angela stand by when the Butt-Uglies were ready to put an end to his existence?

2. Why is Rinco on the list of aliens you would definitely NOT trust with your life?

3. Who almost always wins when the Butt-Uglies are racing their OMABS?

4. What did Emperor Bog call the burger that became his royal pet, and what happened to it?

5. In which Butt-Ugly Martians episode did Do-Wah and the Butt-Uglies think of becoming rock stars?

6. What do you think are Dr. Damage's real ambitions? Does he want to spend the rest of his life dissecting aliens?

7. Why did Shaboom Shaboom try to outwit and destroy the Butt-Ugly Martians? Was she really 'herself'?

8. If your space vehicle developed a fault, which Butt-Ugly Martian would you choose to fix it, and why?

9. Which alien taught the Butt-Uglies that you can't judge someone by the reputation of their species?

10. Where would you find a Dune Walker?

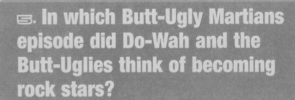

11. What does the Martian word 'grikkies' mean?

12. Name two of Dog's special tech gadgets.

13. Who wanted to dissect Dog in the name of science?

14. What did Dr. Damage create to help Shaboom Shaboom destroy Earth?

15. What is Gorgon's favourite weapon and what does it do?

16. In which Butt-Ugly Martians adventure is Angela reduced to something like tears?

17. How does Humanga arrive on Earth?

18. What device do the Butt-Uglies use to get rid of Gorgon?

19. What skill does Cedric use to defeat Jax?

20. Where would you go if you wanted a night out on the galaxy with a bunch of other aliens?

Q B.Bop: "What do you get if you cross a chicken with Humanga?"

A Do-Wah: "Very big omelettes!"

Q Bog: "Dr. Damage, I keep thinking I'm a bell."

A Damage: "Go back to your bridge, I'll give you a ring later."

Q Cedric: "What goes ha, ha, bonk?"

A Do-Wah: "Damage laughing his head off."

Q How do you get a baby Martian to sleep?

A Rocket...

Q 2-T: "What do you get if you cross Emperor Bog with a skunk?"

A B.Bop: "A creature with even fewer friends."

Butt-Uglies' Rover Pod

Stolen from the Bogstar, this Rover Pod, expertly customised by 2-T, is the Butt-Uglies' pride and joy. So when they're flying through space, the BUMs are fast, super-cool and in control!

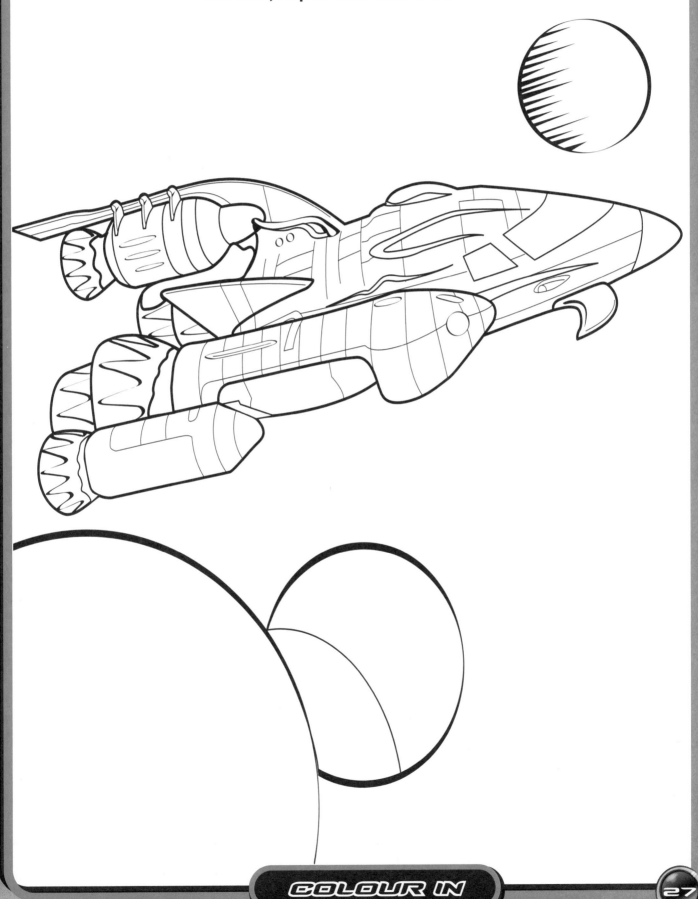

Powers of Observation

Emperor Bog has set the three Butt-Uglies a new challenge to test their powers of observation. He has tampered with a photograph of himself and Dr. Damage on the bridge of the Bogstar. Can you help the Martians to spot ten differences in the picture on the right?

THE ALIENS HAVE JUST BEEN OFFERED 1 MILLION GRIZBUCKS TO BRING IN THE BUTT-UGLY MARTIANS: DEAD OR ALIVE!

THAT'S TOO MUCH MONEY ANYWAY.

THERE ISN'T ENOUGH MONEY IN THE UNIVERSE!

BIG NUMBERS GET US ALL CONFUSED.

CAN YOU BELIEVE THAT GUY? NO WAY AM I TAKING THAT JOB!

LET *HIM* BE HUMILIATED BY THOSE THREE AND SEE HOW HE LIKES IT.

BUT WE KNOW WHAT THEY'RE REALLY THINKING:

I'M GONNA GET THOSE THREE, AND GET THAT MILLION GRIZBUCKS!

FROM MULDOON'S SILO ...

MR. MULDOON! MR. MULDOON!

THE ALIENS ARE COMING!!! THE ALIENS ARE COMING!!!

AT QUANTUM BURGERS ...

MAN, NOTHIN' SAYS 'PARTY' LIKE ...

HE WENT TO QUANTUM BURGERS TO PICK UP THE FOOD.

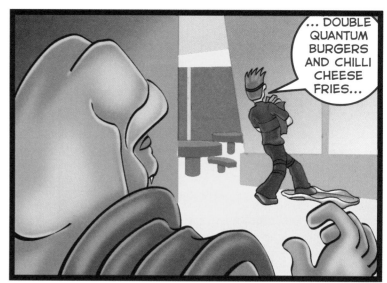

... DOUBLE QUANTUM BURGERS AND CHILLI CHEESE FRIES...

UK!!!!

I LOVE PARTIES, BUT I THINK YOU GUYS FORGOT TO INVITE ME. HA! HA! HA!

BACK AT ZAPZ ...

HEY, GUYS. I'VE GOT THE FOOD!

QUANTUM BURGERS! GIMME!

HEY, HOW OLD ARE THESE BURGERS? WHAT A STINK!

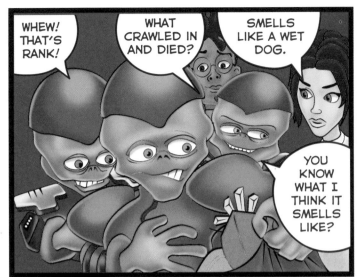

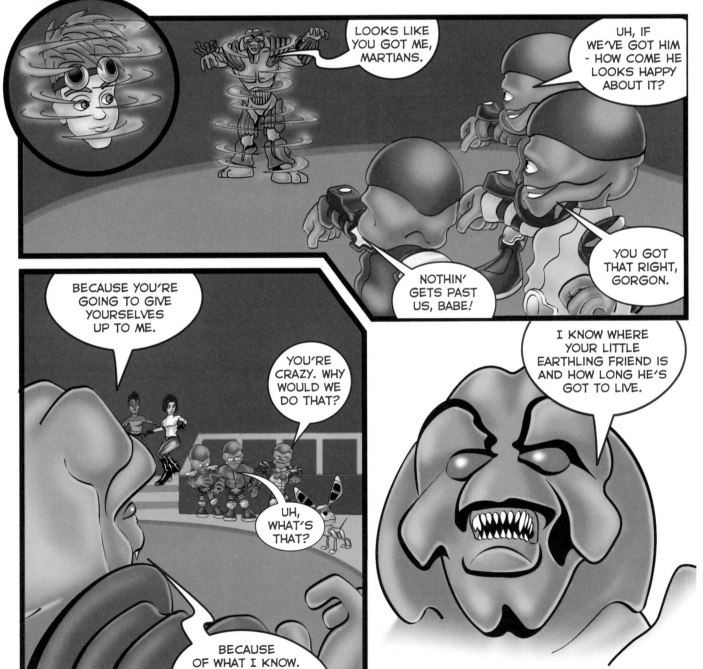

As we all know, Emperor Bog is a kind-hearted, generous individual who loves children and cute, furry aliens... although you would never say so to his face. Doing that would land you somewhere between a dungeon on Pluto and a black hole. The bubbly side of Emperor Bog can be seen nowhere better than in his desire to keep a royal pet of some kind or another at all times. Here are just a few of the, uh, rather surprising pets Emperor Bog has fed and watered over the years.

Mike here again with more info on EB!

INFO-SEEK

SATELLITE RADAR

FILE SEARCH

Fifi

One of Bog's favourite pets was Fifi. Fifi arrived on the end of a broom handle that had been sent to the Bogstar from planet Earth for detailed analysis. During the analysis, Fifi fell off and was thrown into a corner. On an inspection tour Bog found poor Fifi and fell in love with it, especially its hairy tummy. He never found out what the hole on top was for, so he just kept stuffing it with leftovers. He made Fifi his Pet-in-Waiting and had a special hover chair made just for her, or him. The scientists who threw Fifi into the corner were never seen again.

Gumbolt

In the annals of Bog's pets, Gumbolt is way down the list of favourites. Bog was still devastated by the loss of his previous pet when Gumbolt turned up. He was an Earth specimen Damage didn't want. He had a round, wobbly body and eight legs, each of which had suckers on it so Gumbolt could attach himself to things. Bog liked the way his new pet would hold on to his arm – it made him feel wanted. Then things got out of hand. Gumbolt insisted on hanging on to the Emperor's head, especially when he was barking out important orders. Eventually it took several minions to pry Gumbolt loose and with great regret Bog had him fried and served up for lunch.

Kamlix

When the Butt-Ugly Martians sent a horde of Earth stuff as a present for their esteemed emperor, it included a stray quantum burger. Bog immediately established a rapport with the burger and named it as his new royal pet. He called it Kamlix. Emperor Bog grew so fond of Kamlix he hardly ever let it out of his sight. Unfortunately, as time wore on Kamlix wore out and began to go off! Bog got very upset about this and so Kamlix was secretly replaced by another healthier burger!

Pop

Pop came from the planet Urfat and was nothing more than a bubble. However, Bog particularly liked the way it floated about and never answered back. Damage explained that it might be too delicate to withstand hard space flight, and sure enough, one day Pop floated too close to Damage's scalpel whilst he was dissecting a victim...

Wormies

These strange, long, thin creatures lived together in a bowl and swam about in a thick red liquid. Bog spent hours watching the wormies to see if they actually did anything besides sitting in their pool of red stuff. They didn't. After a time Bog became impatient and ordered Damage to look at them closely. When the doctor's face loomed over the useless wormies, Bog lost his cool and slammed his fist down on the bowl. The mess of wormies was launched upwards into Damage's evil features. At last the wormies had done something to amuse their master!

All aboard the OMABs!

LET'S GET UGLY!

COLOUR IN

WELCOME to the HOVERBOARD PARK GAME

Cedric, Mike and Angela spend their spare moments – when they're not having adventures with aliens – practising awesome stunts down on the Hoverboard Park. With all the best wheels, tunnels and ramps, it really is the coolest pace to hang out! So grab a couple of friends, and join the kids as you show off your speed and tricky manoeuvres in the game on the next page.

How to play

YOU WILL NEED:

Counters for up to 4 players **(see page 93)**; dice

1 Cut out or copy the counter pieces on page 93 (or use your own if you prefer) and place them on position 1 at the start of the game.

2 Roll the dice to decide who moves first. The highest number starts.

3 Taking it in turns, move your counter according to what you roll on the dice, following the numbers in sequence. You'll move through all the obstacles in the park, including the tube, the high tube, the super slot and the loop. The larger, numbered positions require extra activities – you'll either be rewarded for a fantastic stunt, or sent back for crashing! If you are instructed to go back to the FIRST AID STATION, start again from position 12 on your next go.

4 The first player to hover successfully to the finish position is the winner! So get ready to pop your tail and gli-i-i-ide!

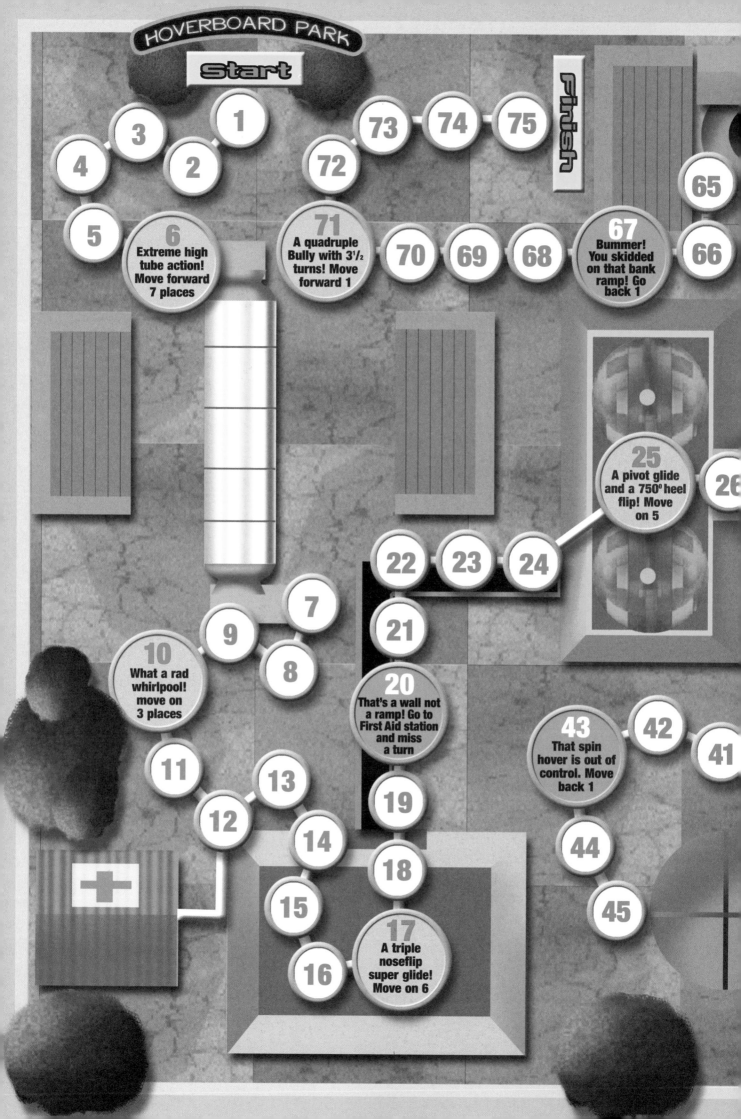

GALACTIC GAGS

WARNING! MARTIAN JOKES

Q What does Dog enjoy chasing on Earth?

A Catfish...

What did 2-T call his over-sized computer mouse?
*
A hippopotomouse.

Do-Wah found half-a-dozen milk bottles in a field the other day.
*
He thought it was a cow's nest!

DOWNLOADING 85%

Q How does the vet examine Dog's teeth?

A Very carefully.

Knock, knock!
Who's there?
Harry.
Harry who?
Harry up and get out of there –
Humanga's behind you.

Q Cedric: "Do you have kangaroos on Mars?"

A B.Bop: 'Yeah, they are called Mars-upials..."

Q 2T: "Why do Earth birds fly south for the winter?"

A Angela: "Because it's too far to walk."

BUTT-UGLY MARTIANS

PIN-UP

STOAT MULDOON

PIN·UP

BUT·UGLY MARTIANS ™

MULDOON'S HOVERVAN

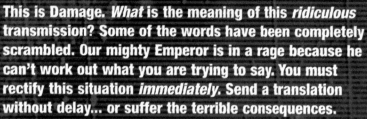

This is Damage. *What* is the meaning of this *ridiculous* transmission? Some of the words have been completely scrambled. Our mighty Emperor is in a rage because he can't work out what you are trying to say. You must rectify this situation *immediately*. Send a translation without delay... or suffer the terrible consequences.

BEG PER ROOM!

Tomorrow we are sending you a tribute from Earth.
This will include: a BRAVO HORDE,
RODEO CAM 2000 and a QUART GRUB MENU.
We are also sending some Earthworms for RAD MADGE.
(They taste even better than TWO-ARM SLOB.)

Are you experiencing an equipment meltdown?
Why isn't your Tech Commando doing his job properly?
What has happened to this transmission?
It looks as if the letters B, J, K, P and X
have been added at random.
An urgent re-transmission is required.
Emperor Bog is about to blow his stack!

BJCXPOMKINBJGX SPJOKONB: TKHJEPB
LKABTPEXSKTB VXIBDJEKOPJKS XOPFK
JOBUXRP PSJKUXBCBCPEKSJJSPFBUL
XCPONBQUXPESTJ KBOF KEPABRTXHJ.
BJWIKTNBESS XFBIKRPEB,
BDJEPKSBTXRUBCJTIPJONX AXNBDP
JDKIPSJAXSBTKEPRP. BSXEJE PTHEB
JEAXRPTBHKLIBNJGKSP BSXUBFJFPEXKRB!

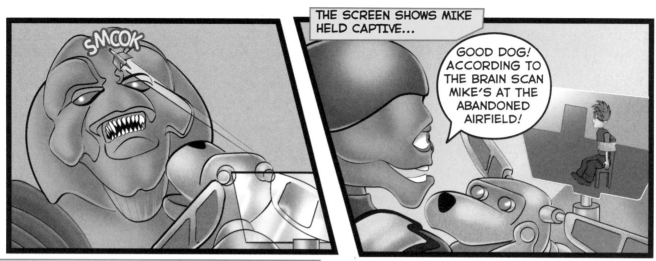

SMCOK

THE SCREEN SHOWS MIKE HELD CAPTIVE...

GOOD DOG! ACCORDING TO THE BRAIN SCAN MIKE'S AT THE ABANDONED AIRFIELD!

AT THE ABANDONED AIRFIELD, MOMENTS LATER...

THANK GOODNESS YOU'RE OKAY. THE MARTIANS WERE REALLY WORRIED.

HEY, WHERE ARE THEY ANYWAY?

WAITING FOR MY SIGNAL.

MIKE'S OKAY, GUYS.

SO LET'S LIGHT THIS CANDLE

... AND GET BACK TO THE PARTY.

FIRE ONE, DOG!

I'LL BE BAAAAAAAACK!!

WHOOSH

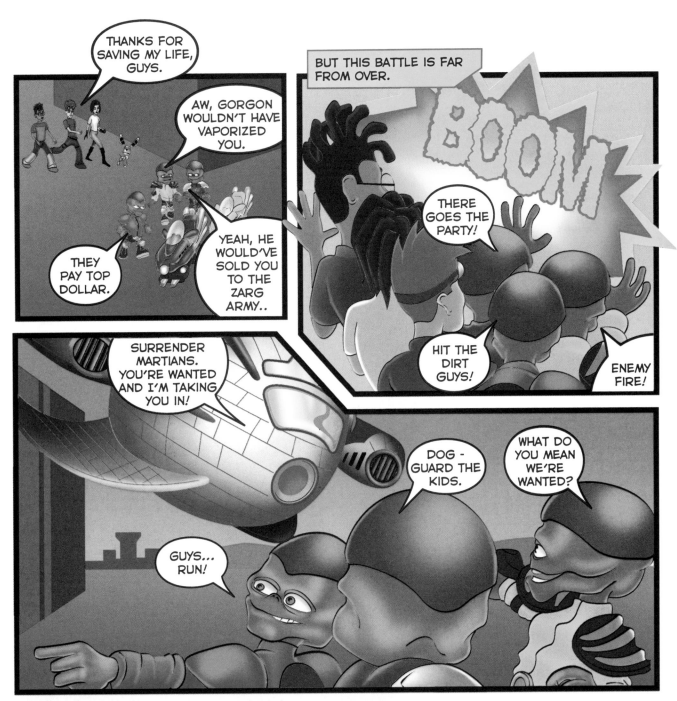

STOAT'S QUOTES

INCOMING TRANSMISSION

"Here is a sample of some of the very strange things that have gone on in the world this year. Some of them might even involve the nasty alien scum I keep telling you about. Others are the work of some very odd minds..."

Q. I often stay up late at night. Sometimes in our upstairs hallway I see a shadow with a long flowing robe and tubes for hair. Could this be the shadow of an alien? If it is, what should I do? I'm not a professional alien hunter of course.
Orville Drone

A. Luckily, however, I AM a professional alien hunter, as well as being a TV and internet personality. This could be an alien sighting of great significance to the people of this planet — or it could be your older sister. Sometimes, I am told, older sisters go to bed with strange attachments linked to their heads. On the other hand, you could be in big trouble if your house has been taken over by a horde of strangely quiet aliens! Let me know if you have an older sister. If you don't, I'll be right around. Uh, and if you do I might be right around anyway.

Q. What can I do? My pet cat Hubert has been taken over by an alien entity. He talks in a language I don't understand and glows in the dark. My dad is scared of him and won't come down out of the loft until I provide him with a suitable explanation. Can you help?
Irene Plungetoken

A. Miss Plungetoken, has your cat ever been close to a nuclear establishment? I believe this might account for the glowing. Mind you, that wouldn't explain the speaking in a different language problem. In my vast and untapped experience, I would say your cat may well be the victim of an alien take-over — much like when Great Uncle Gilbert's ice cream business was taken over by Ben and Gerbil's in 2021. You must beware; he may be about to hatch a plot to take over the Earth. Keep a lookout for other glowing cats, too. In the meantime, use him as a lamp in the living room to save electricity. Aliens can sometimes have their uses...

Q. I watched your show the other week and I don't know whether it is a comedy or not. My mom laughs from beginning to end, but I just don't see the funny side. Tarquin Inem

A. Tarquin, my show is not, I repeat, not a comedy. It is a piece of serious investigative journalism carried out by my good self. Securing our precious Earth from Alien scum invaders is no laughing matter! Your mom should be ashamed of herself. Aliens are a dangerous and slippery breed. I should know because of the many I have not managed to catch yet. But I'm trying. Look closely at your Mother. Does she show any signs of shape shifting? Does a leg or arm occasionally fall off only for her to hastily replace it? If so, even she could be an alien. You can never be too sure... get a photo of her and then hightail it outta there. Once we have that all-important photo, we can finally prove that THEY are here.

Q. Last night I passed by a warehouse with a bunch of large barrels in front. I'm sure I saw one of them move! As the warehouse is close to a flat, open space where aliens could land, I'm convinced that's what the barrels contain. Should I contact the authorities?

A. I AM "the authorities" when it comes to aliens, you young whippersnapper, and don't you forget it! However, in this case I can't be sure... It reminds me of the Barundian oil drum affair in which I unfortunately mistook some barrels for aliens. I know it cost the US government millions of dollars but I still maintain that I wasn't responsible for bringing all the vehicles in Los Angeles to a halt for a full week. So I suggest you leave the barrels alone!

Q. I think I've been abducted, but no-one will believe my story. Can you help me? I seem to remember little blue men and this odd-looking jerk who kept talking about conquering the Earth and dissecting me. My parents think I'm having bad dreams but I believe I was abducted. What's your opinion?
Derek Hyperbole

A. Derek, no wonder no-one believes your story! Who ever heard of little blue men? And as for all that dissection stuff, I suggest you don't eat anything before going to bed. It can upset your delicate system and cause nightmares of the type you mention. Young people of today should maintain a healthy diet and lifestyle, just like yours truly, Number One Alien Hunter.

Q. My granny, Nelly Underspear, is well known for her super-strength hydrogen haggis. It is very nutritional and is also able to power solid fuel rockets! Do you think Grandma's haggis could be used in the fight against alien scum? I can supply it to you for a reduced price…
Buzz Underspear

A. Buzz, I am all in favour of healthy eating practices, especially for young persons, and of using the most up-to-date, high-tech apparatus for fighting the alien menace. Therefore, I am sure your Grandma Nelly's hydrogen haggis will prove more than useful. Could you send several cases to my headquarters in the Mojave Desert. I have an idea for an anti-alien hydrogen haggis bomb. Send the bill later.

ILLEGAL USER

49

ANGELA

Angela is Mike's neighbour and best friend. She's known him all her life and tends to treat him like a younger brother, although her affection for him may well take another direction as time passes.

2 for 1

»An all-round cyber babe, Angela may appear to be a tomboy, but she's not, as anyone who dares to suggest will be told in no uncertain terms! Angela's tongue can be as sharp as her brain, but she is sassy, cool and fun to hang out with.

» Once she understood the Butt-Uglies and what they were about, Angela became very fond of them. She sees them as special

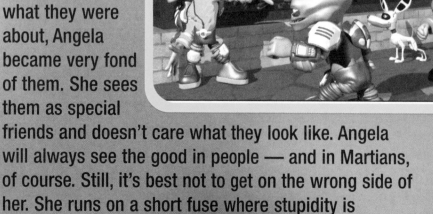

friends and doesn't care what they look like. Angela will always see the good in people — and in Martians, of course. Still, it's best not to get on the wrong side of her. She runs on a short fuse where stupidity is concerned and says exactly what she thinks.

At home, Angela likes to read and to watch TV, especially documentaries, sport and drama. She uses the internet to help with her studies and is a straight 'A' student, much to the disgust of Mike.

This cyber babe can also cook and is well known for her fish and feathers barbecues. Cedric once ate five haddock and a half a chicken at one sitting! He couldn't get on his hoverboard for the rest of the day... Angela showed him no sympathy at all!

Angela's Helmet

Angela is also brave and adventurous. Her hoverboard skills are almost as good as Mike's, and she won't back down when faced with a challenge or a crisis. It was Angela who insisted that the kids help the Martians when they were about to be annihilated by Stoat Muldoon. She also acts as the voice of reason and good sense when the other two hotheads are about to do something brave but not too clever.

Angela's Board

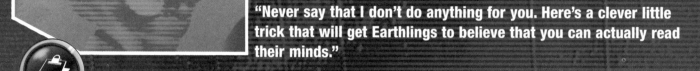

"Never say that I don't do anything for you. Here's a clever little trick that will get Earthlings to believe that you can actually read their minds."

Ask the Earthling to think of a number between 1 and 10.

Then say:

"Add 5, take away 3, add 7, add 2.

Take away the number you first thought of.

Your answer is … 11!"

You can use any numbers for this trick. Just keep track of the sum in your head. When the dim-witted Earthlings take away their first number, they'll be left with your answer.

Here's another trick that will dumbfound those simpletons on Earth.

Tell the Earthlings to

think of a number between 2 and 1,000

Let's say they choose 247

Ask them to multiply the number by 9

(They can use a pen and paper for this if they're too dense to do it in their heads.)

$$247 \times 9 = 2223$$

Then get them to tell you the answer, but with one of the numerals missing.

If they say 223, for example, you can easily tell them that a 2 is missing.

That's because if you multiply any number by nine, the numerals of the answer will always add up to 9 or 18:

$$2 + 2 + 2 + 3 = 9$$

EMPEROR BOG

BUTT-UGLY MARTIANS™

PIN·UP

PIN-UP

BUT-UGLY MARTIANS™

BOOSTAR and Alien Fleet

"I need to test your GAK (General Alien Knowledge) levels before I can accept you for further training. Can you unscramble the letters in each of the sections below to find the names of some evil alien scum? In the middle section, two names have been scrambled together."

W A D H O D D Y I O D

Write your answer here

Write your answer here

B L O B N P U A A

A E A M D G D R

O O K G R R O N K G T A L

Write your answer here

Write your answer here

Write your answer here

A N U G A H M

O M B E P O G R E R

Write your answer here

Write your answer here

THE MARTIANS FIND THEMSELVES IN A NASTY SITUATION. AGAIN!

OUR GRIKKIES ARE TOAST!!!

I CHOOSE LIFE.

BUT WE'RE SURROUNDED. WHAT CAN WE DO?

WE'VE GOT TO GET THE KIDS OUT OF HERE.

YOU'RE RIGHT, ONE STRAY BOOGER BLAST FROM THE KARSCH BROTHERS AND THEY'RE A MEMORY.

NOW THAT'S A GREAT IDEA!

WE COULD SURRENDER.

GOOD GOING, BABE.

UH... REALLY?

Hoverboards

The kids love nothing more than getting on their hoverboards and pulling off some cool moves. Bring their triple noseflip superglides and 720⁰ shrakwhakers to life by adding your own rad colours!

COLOUR IN

BUTT-UGLY MARTIANS™

PIN-UP

©2000 Just Entertainment Ltd./
Mike Young Productions Inc.
Licensed by Just Licensing Ltd.

Cedric   Angela   Mikey

Cedric

Pin-up

Angela

Mikey

FUTURE PUZZLES

"If you want to be part of my team, you'll need to be really clear about who are our friends and who are our enemies. Circle the alien names in this grid in red, and the human names in blue."

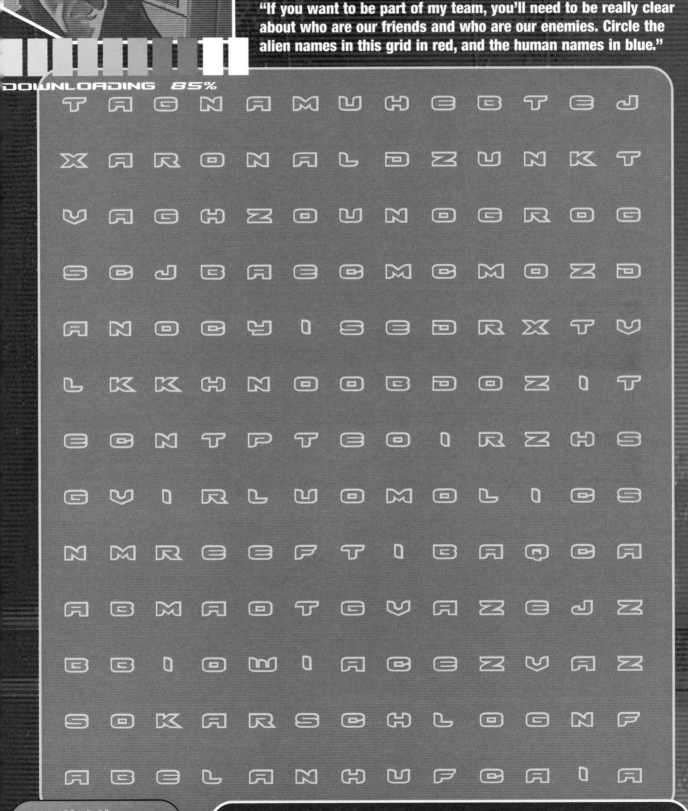

Hot tip:
Names can read up, down, diagonally, backwards and forwards.

NAMES TO FIND

Bobb, Ronald, Fleaboid, Koofoo, Jax, Rinko, Angela, Mike, Cedric, Karsch, Gorgon, Chitzok, Humanga

CEDRIC

Cedric can always be found hanging out with his best buddies, Mike and Angela, and now the Butt-Ugly Martians. He is a year younger than Mike and Angela, but is easily their equal in the brains department. He skipped a couple of grades in school and that's why he is friends with the older pair.

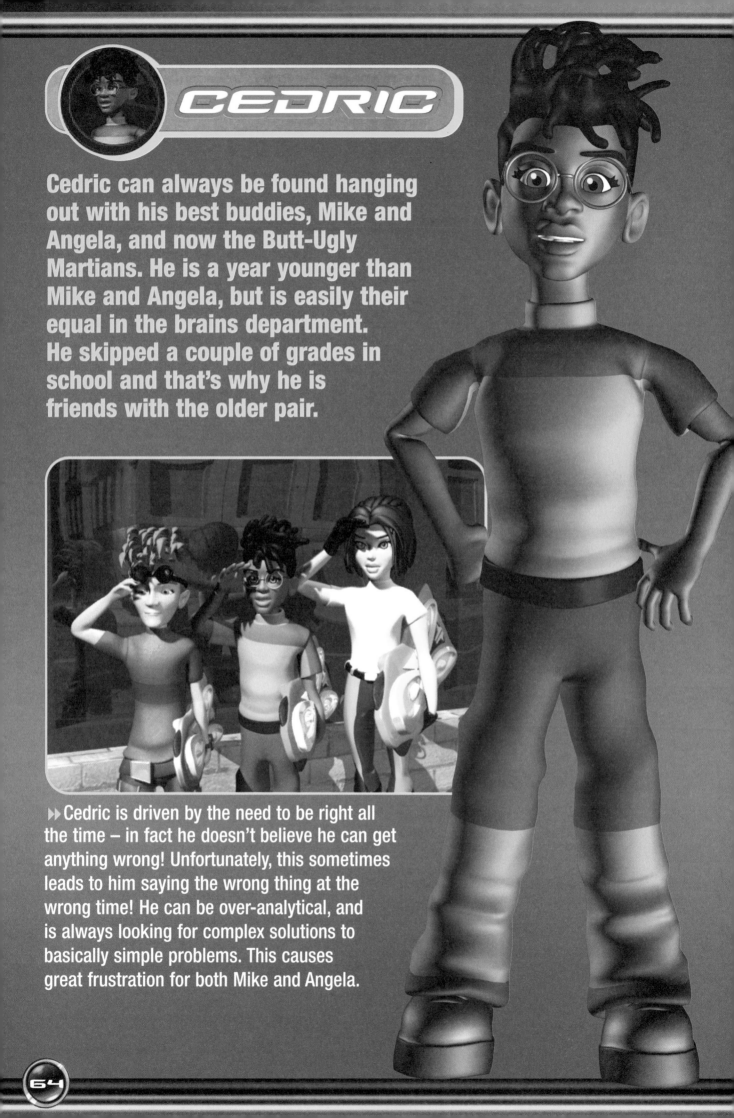

▶▶Cedric is driven by the need to be right all the time – in fact he doesn't believe he can get anything wrong! Unfortunately, this sometimes leads to him saying the wrong thing at the wrong time! He can be over-analytical, and is always looking for complex solutions to basically simple problems. This causes great frustration for both Mike and Angela.

Cedric's Board

Cedric's Helmet

QUANTUM BURGERS

▶▶ Cedric loves his Martian friends, but this doesn't stop him trying to make a quick buck off them whenever he can. This is especially true where their technology is concerned. Give Cedric an interesting "toy" and he'll try and find a way to market it. His parents worry about his behaviour and try to get him to do more kid-like things, such as reading comics or watching cartoons.

▶▶ Cedric loves cheesemongers and adventure!

▶▶ Cedric has a brain like a computer when it comes to finding out the value of something. He loves to sit at home and browse through the Financial Times, as well as checking out the stock market read-outs on the Net and on TV.

1. Which of Damage's creations can rebuild itself automatically?

2. When asked by Damage, how does Mike describe a basketball?

3. What does Shaboom Shaboom use to negate the Butt-Uglies' BKM mode?

4. Where does Stoat Muldoon make his headquarters?

5. Has Muldoon ever caught an alien himself?

6. Who is Ronald the counter jerk's alter ego?

7. How do the Butt-Uglies deal with their constant interaction with Stoat Muldoon?

8. Which Butt-Ugly Martian is as strong as the other two put together?

9. How do most vehicles get about in 2053?

10. What weapons do Bog's minions carry with them?

11. What happens to Dog's eyes when he is in broadcast mode?

12. What vehicle did 2-T create that is 12 feet tall and has long robotic arms?

13. Who designed the Bogstar?

14. What does OMAB stand for?

15. Which alien has devised a machine that can literally quake Earth into submission, and what is it called?

16. What is the special body weapon used by the Karsh twins?

17. Who holds the Doomrace 2000 points record?

18. What is the weird connection between the Karsh twins, Bobb and Fleaboid, that can also be used as a punishment?

19. How did Dr. Damage get rid of Prince Netzor?

20. How can you tell if the alien shape shifter Gorgon is around even if you can't see him?

LIFE ON MARS

Mars is the fourth planet from the Sun in the solar system. It is often called the Red Planet, because it is covered in red rocks and dust and gives off a red glow in the night sky. Mars is half the size of Earth and being further away from the Sun, its surface temperature is much lower – it is well below freezing most of the time. The thin atmosphere on Mars consists mainly of carbon dioxide and is unbreathable.

Rock on

▸▸ The surface of Mars is covered with rocks and dust. These appear as light and dark patches. The lighter areas cover about two-thirds of the surface.

Mars has two natural satellites, the moons Phobos and Deimos

Ice caps

▸▸ The planet's poles contain ice caps. These are believed to be frozen carbon dioxide. The ice caps grow larger in winter, as extreme cold causes more carbon dioxide to freeze. They shrink in the summer, when rising temperatures cause the carbon dioxide to melt.

home sweet home ...

Mars's vital statistics

Diameter at the equator is 6,794 kilometres

Distance from the Sun is 227,940,000 kilometres

Nearest distance to Earth is 78,390,000 kilometres

Orbits the Sun in 686.980 days

Rotates on its axis (once) in 24 hours, 37 minutes, 22.6 seconds

Highest temperature is 31°C

Lowest temperature is ¯124°C

Atmosphere is made up of carbon dioxide, with some nitrogen and argon, and traces of oxygen

Seasons on Mars are twice as long as on Earth

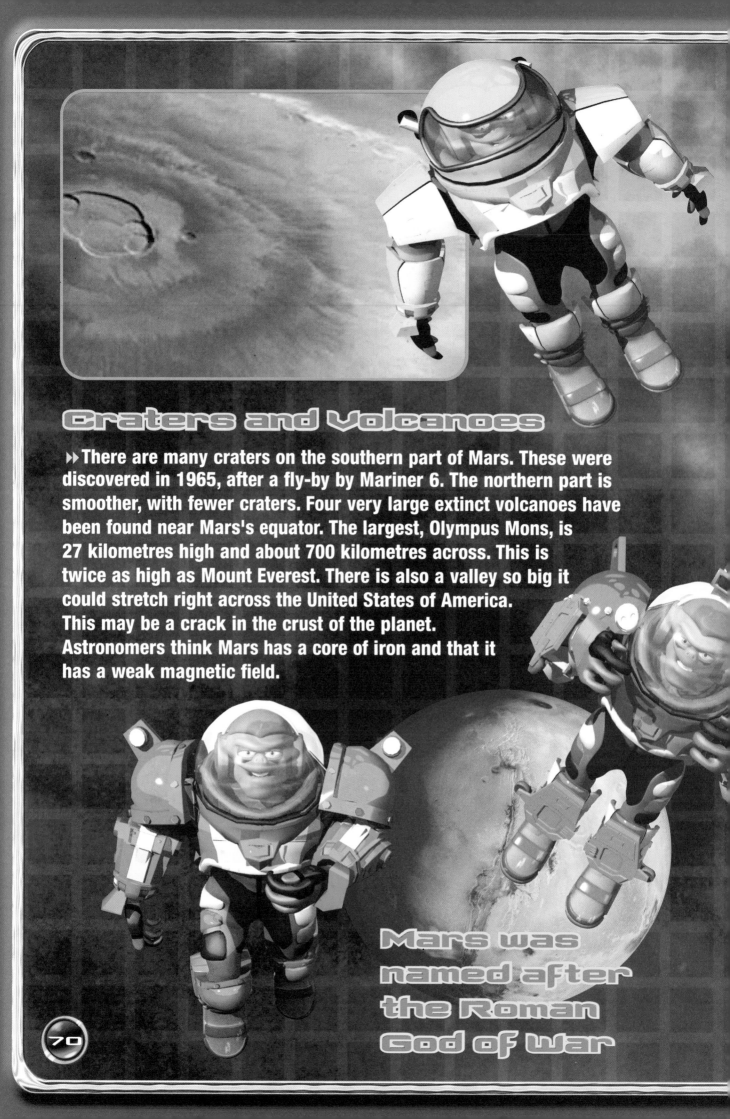

Craters and Volcanoes

▸▸ There are many craters on the southern part of Mars. These were discovered in 1965, after a fly-by by Mariner 6. The northern part is smoother, with fewer craters. Four very large extinct volcanoes have been found near Mars's equator. The largest, Olympus Mons, is 27 kilometres high and about 700 kilometres across. This is twice as high as Mount Everest. There is also a valley so big it could stretch right across the United States of America. This may be a crack in the crust of the planet. Astronomers think Mars has a core of iron and that it has a weak magnetic field.

Mars was named after the Roman God of War

Spacecraft

Mariner 4

▶▶ Mariner 4 was the first successful spacecraft voyage to the Red Planet. It was launched in 1964 on a 228-day mission to collect planetary science data.

2001 Mars Odyssey

▶▶ The Mars Odyssey was launched on April 7th, 2001, and is due to arrive at Mars in October 2001. It will map minerals and elements, look for water, and study the radiation environment of the planet.

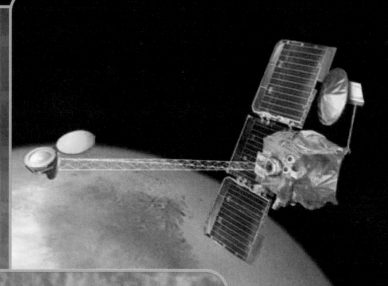

2003 Rover

▶▶ NASA plans to send twin Mars Exploration Rovers to the Red Planet in 2003–2004. This is an artist's rendering of the space vehicle. Its landing will be cushioned by airbags.

STAND YOUR GROUND YOU... UH, WHATEVER-YOU-TWO-ARE... THE MARTIANS ARE NO MATCH FOR OUR MIGHT!

THEY "MIGHT" TRY AND WHUMP US, BUT WE MIGHT KICK THEIR...

MIGHT WHAT?

WOOSHH

FLABOOMAA!!

FLASH

... THE IMPACT CAN BE FELT FOR MILES. ALL THE WAY TO...

... THE HOME OF STOAT MULDOON: ALIEN HUNTER!

HUNGA-BUNGA!

ALIEN ALERT

IT'S AN ALIEN INVASION! RONALD! WHY DIDN'T YOU TELL ME?

ALIEN ALERT

RONALD?

THE BATTLE BEGINS!

GRRRRR!!!!

HAH! YOU FELLAS DON'T STAND A CHANCE!

LET'S TENDERIZE 'EM BEFORE WE TURN 'EM IN, FLEABOID.

SOUNDS LIKE FUN, BOBB.

BOBB 'N' ME BEEN RASSLIN' SINCE WE WUZ LITTLE PUPZOIDS!

SLAM

DON'T WORRY, GUYS, HELP'S ON THE WAY!

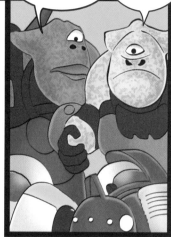

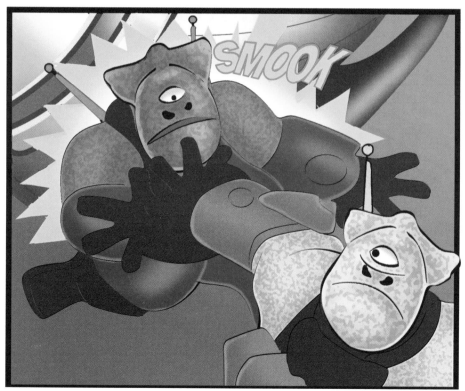

SMOOK

WAY TO GO, DO-WAH!

THEY'RE OUT OF TROUBLE NOW!

UH, NO THEY'RE NOT.

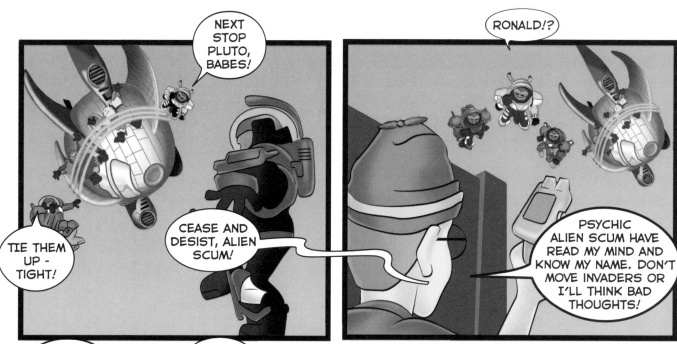

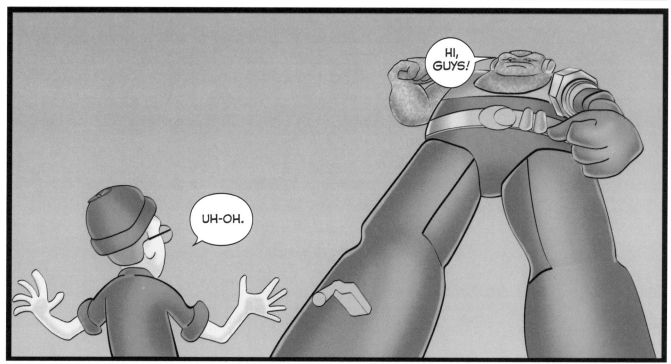

GALACTIC GAGS

WARNING! MARTIAN JOKES

Q What does 2-T stand for?

A Bloatworms on the top shelf

Q What do you get if you cross Gorgon with a hamster?

A A very smelly cage…

Why does Do-Wah need glasses?
*
Because he keeps on making a spectacle of himself.

Q What do you get if Humanga sits on your piano?

A A bunch of flat notes…

Q Mike: What flag does Emperor Bog fly when he's in battle?

A B.Bop: The Bog Standard

BUTT-UGLY MARTIANS

PIN-UP

©2000 Just Entertainment Ltd./
Mike Young Productions Inc.
Licensed by Just Licensing Ltd.

Jax

BUTT-UGLY MARTIANS

Pin-Up

©2000 Just Entertainment Ltd./
Mike Young Productions Inc.
Licensed by Just Licensing Ltd.

KLAKTOR

DOWNLOADING 90%

"Quickly! Here's your chance to prove yourself as a serious alien eradicator. These lights flashing on my MATD screen show where aliens are lurking. If we intercept this message, it could lead us straight to them. Hurry! We must block their escape route."

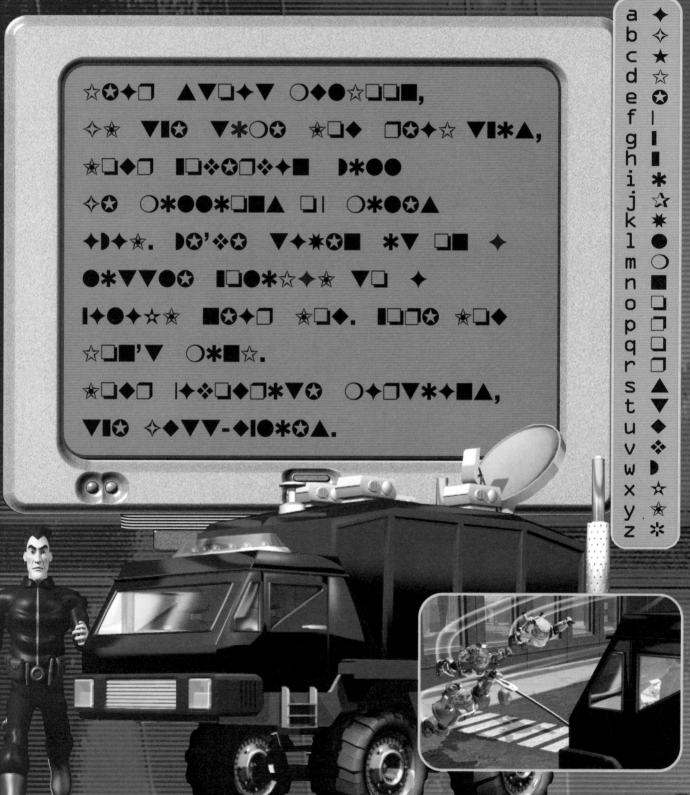

BUT I SAW YOU PULL THE SAME TRICK ON JAX AND THE KARSCH BROTHERS.

AND THE REWARD'S A MILLION GRIZBUCKS ALIVE... OR DEAD! HA-HA-HA!

WHAM

HE BEAT THE MARTIANS!

THEY'RE GONE...

...FOREVER.

LATER, AT THE ALIEN CANTINA.

YOU DID IT! OH, JOY! OH, UNMITIGATED DELIGHT!

THAT'LL BE A MILLION GRIZBUCKS, BUDDY.

YOU'LL GET IT. WITH THOSE THREE GONE THE EARTH INVASION WILL FAIL. BOG WILL LOSE FAVOUR. I'LL TAKE OVER THE MARTIAN EMPIRE AND PAY YOU FROM THE MARTIAN TREASURY.

21st CENTURY PRIZES

2nd prize

2-T's SPOOF VIDEO

BUTT-UGLY MARTIANS

2-T'S QUIZ BOOK

BUTT-UGLY MARTIANS
The Martians have landed!

DVD

SPECIAL FEATURES ON DVD
DVD INCLUDES:
Interactive Games
Photo Gallery
Exclusive Comic Strip
Behind-The-Scenes Interviews
Bonus Trailers

OH GRIX
PG

WIN!

Books, DVDs, videos, trading cards, figurines – this goody-bag contains everything you could possibly want for the ultimate Butt-Ugly experience

THE TELEPORTER HAS SENT UP SEVERAL EARTH THINGS I HAVE NO USE FOR. SO OUT OF THE GOODNESS OF MY HEART (YES I DO HAVE ONE), I'M GIVING THEM AWAY. ANSWER THIS DEVILISHLY DIFFICULT QUESTION CORRECTLY AND THE EARTH ITEMS WILL BE YOURS. ANSWER IT WRONG AND YOU'LL BE SCRUBBING DOWN MY OPERATING TABLE FOR A MONTH.

WHICH OF BOG'S PETS ENDED UP CLOSER TO ME THAN TO HIM?

84

1st prize

3rd prize

WIN!

This fantastic DVD player will bring digital quality sound and pictures to your own home cinema... enjoy your favourite Butt-Ugly moments, plus interative games, behind-the-scenes interviews, and more!

WIN!

A collection of Butt-Ugly adventures on video. The accident-prone martians and their Earthling pals star in the best episodes from the hit TV show!

BUTT-UGLY MARTIANS™

DOG RESCUE!

INSIDE ZAPZ ARCADE, 2-T'S PECKISH AS USUAL...

WOW, ALL THAT FAKE BATTLE REPORTING TO EMPEROR BOG HAS MADE ME HUMANGOUSLY HUNGRY! I NEED A BURGER FIX.

BUT WE'LL BE SEEN. THEN AGAIN... THE COUNTER GUY IS A REAL JERK SO MAYBE WE CAN RIDE UP TO THE DRIVE-THROUGH AND WE'LL BE OUT BEFORE HE REALISES WHAT'S GOING ON. LET'S HIT THE OMABS!

AT QUANTUM BURGERS DRIVE-THROUGH, 2-T'S GETTING CARRIED AWAY...

I CAN'T WAIT TO GET MY HANDS ON A DOZEN QUANTUM BURGERS!

TAKE IT EASY RUMBLE GUTS, WE WON'T HAVE TIME. A COUPLE OF BURGERS AND SOME FRIES EACH, OKAY?

AND A BAG OF SQUIGGLY-WIGS FOR DOG. HA, HA, HA...

SCREEECH!

6 QUANTUM BURGERS, 6 CHILLI FRIES, 6 ECOCOLAS, HOLD THE BLOATWORMS. OOPS!

WHAT'S THAT? BLOATWORMS... IS THIS A JOKE? I'D BETTER HAVE A LOOK.

EEEEEEEEK! IT'S ALIENS - OR A MOBILE FANCY DRESS BALL.

NO, IT'S DEFINITELY ALIENS. ALIENS HAVE LANDED...

GOT TO CALL THE GREAT MAN HIMSELF, STOAT MULDOON, ALIEN HUNTER!

CALM DOWN, YOUNG HASH SLINGER.

BLUE CREATURES ON SUPER BIKES? HOLD THEM THERE, THOSE ALIEN SCUM WON'T GET AWAY!

THE OPERATION'S LOOKING RISKY...

CAN'T WAIT. I GOTTA EAT MINE RIGHT NOW.

COME ON MAN, WE GOTTA GET OUT BEFORE WE'RE SPOTTED

JUST EAT ONE. SAVE THE REST 'TIL WE GET BACK.

Munch!

Krunch!

Brrrrum!

Burp!

MULDOON IS ON HIS WAY AND ON THE CASE...

MULDOON HAS ARRIVED. NOW, WHERE ARE THOSE PESKY...? HOLY MOTHER MCREADY, REAL ALIENS!

HOLD IT LITTLE BLUE ALIEN PERSONS. YOU CAN'T ESCAPE ME NOW. I'VE GOT YOU!

STOP THAT MUNCHING AND PUT YOUR HANDS UP... OR WHATEVER OTHER ALIEN DIGIT HOLDING APPENDAGES YOU MAY HAVE EVOLVED.

OH NO! IT'S THAT ALIEN-HUNTING HONCHO AGAIN.

TIME TO BE SOMEWHERE ELSE FOLKS...

HE'S GETTING CLOSE. DOG - DECOY MODE. GIVE US SOME TIME TO GET OUT OF THESE NARROW STREETS.

WOOF, WOOF, YARP, BLEEP!

SCREEECH!

HOLY SMOKE, IT'S THAT DIGITAL DOG AGAIN! BUT THIS TIME IT WON'T ESCAPE. NOT FROM STOAT MULDOON, ALIEN DOG CATCHER.

SECONDS LATER DOG FINDS HIMSELF IN STOAT'S ALIEN DOG CATCHING NET.

STRANGE MONGREL - PART MASTIFF, PART HAIRLESS CHIHUAHUA, PART TOASTER. EASY BOY...

WOOF, WOOF, BLEEP.

MEANWHILE BACK AT ZAPZ

IN MY NEXT PROGRAMME I HAVE SOMETHING VERY SPECIAL TO SHOW YOU- THE WORKING PARTS OF AN ALIEN CANINE.

OH NO! DOG'S A DEAD DUCK!

TAKE IT EASY, WE'LL GET HIM BACK.

WE'D BETTER MAKE SURE MULDOON DOESN'T SEE US COMING.

STAY UNDER HIS SCANNER BEAMS. THEN HIDE BESIDE THOSE MOUNDS.

AS THE KIDS APPROACH HIS SECRET BASE, MULDOON IS ABOUT TO BEGIN THE DE-CONSTRUCTION OF DOG...

WELL MY SMALL MECHANICAL MUTT, I WONDER WHAT HAPPENS WHEN WE REMOVE THIS EAR? HMM, HIS BACK HAS OPENED UP.

88

YEAH, CIVILISED PEOPLE WOULD NEVER BEHAVE LIKE THAT!

WE'VE GOT TO GET DOG BACK. MULDOON CAN'T DISSECT HIM. IT'S BARBARIC.

OKAY MARTIANS, NOW I'M MAD. I WON'T STAND FOR DISSECTION.

TIME IS RUNNING OUT...

C'MON LET'S GET IN THERE.

WAIT! IF YOU SCARE MULDOON HE MIGHT DESTROY DOG - COMPLETELY!

OH YEAH, YOU GOT A PLAN?

STAY COOL GUYS. WE'LL GET DOG OUT.

WE NEED TO GET MULDOON OUT SO WE CAN SNEAK IN. YOU GUYS WALK TOWARDS THE BASE SO HIS SCANNER PICKS YOU UP. WHEN HE COMES OUT, WE'LL GET IN. JUST *DON'T* GET CAUGHT.

INSIDE HIS CONTROL ROOM MULDOON SPOTS SOMETHING ON HIS ALIEN DETECTOR

HOLY MOLLY, OL' CHROME YELLER WILL HAVE TO WAIT. THE ALIEN DETECTOR IS PICKING UP SOMETHING.

I KNOW THERE'S SOMETHING OUT THERE - THE TRUTH PERHAPS? **NO, IT'S ALIENS!**

STAND WHERE YOU ARE ALIEN FIENDS. MULDOON HAS YOU COVERED. OH.... WHO? ERM...WHAT?

MULDOON HAS FOUND THE WRONG 'ALIENS'

YOU'RE NOT ALIENS. YOU'RE EARTH KIDS. THANK GOODNESS, UH, I MEAN WHAT A DISAPPOINTMENT.

I THINK YOUR NASTY ALIENS ARE OVER THERE.

GOOD OF YOU TO POINT THAT OUT. AH-HA, SMALL BLUE ALIENS WITH NASTY SMIRKS ON THEIR NOT-TOO-PRETTY FACES.

WAS THIS THE PLAN?

I DON'T THINK SO.

ONLY ONE THING TO DO

AAH-OOH-GAH!

B!

K!

M!

LET'S GET UGLY!

NOW WE'RE GOING TO GET INSIDE THAT BASE - OUR WAY!

HANG IN THERE DOG. WE'RE COMING TO GET YOU!

ZAP!

ZAP!

ZAP!

KRAK-A-BOOM!

DOG'S BACK AND MULDOON'S OUT FOR THE COUNT.

WHA HAPPEN...

BACK AT ZAPZ, EXPLANATIONS ARE REQUIRED...

ONCE DOG WAS FREE WE USED HIS REPLICATOR HOSE TO PUT EVERYTHING BACK TOGETHER AGAIN, JUST AS IT WAS.

AND WE TREATED MULDOON TO A LITTLE MARTIAN MEMORY ERASE PYRAMID - SO HE WON'T REMEMBER A THING!

NOW CAN I HAVE MY OTHER BURGER?

END

Page 10

Answer: martian

Page 11

Answers: 50

```
2 1 2 5
2 1 4 1
3 1 3 3
8 5 5 5
```

Page 16

Pages 24-25

ANSWERS - TEST YOUR GAK

1. Koofoo
2. He'd kill you to win a bet
3. B.Bop
4. Kamlix. It went off and shrivelled up, and was replaced by a fresh burger
5. Out of Sync
6. No, he wants to de-throne Emperor Bog
7. She had been programmed by Damage with a 'mind probe'
8. 2-T, because he's the Tech Commando
9. Koofoo
10. In the desert
11. "Things"
12. Replicator hose, communications screen
13. Dr Brady Hacksaw
14. A Destructor Robot
15. An Energy Bola that he swings around his head and lets loose like a sling
16. That's No Puddle…
17. He rolled in WITHOUT a spaceship
18. A molecular de-atomiser
19. His hoop skill
20. The alien cantina

Page 43

Transmission 1:

EMPEROR BOG!
Tomorrow we are sending you a tribute from Earth. This will include: a HOVERBOARD, DOOMRACE 2000 and a QUANTUM BURGER. We are also sending some Earthworms for DR. DAMAGE. (They taste even better than BLOATWORMS.)

Transmission 2:

COMING SOON:
THE LATEST VIDEOS OF OUR SUCCESSFUL CONQUEST OF EARTH. WITNESS FIRE, DESTRUCTION AND DISASTER. SEE THE EARTHLINGS SUFFER!

Page 55

Answers:
Clockwise from top:

Do-Wah Diddy	B.Bop-a-Luna
Dr. Damage	**Centre:**
Emperor Bog	Klaktor
Humanga	Gorgon

```
1  2  3  4  5  6  7  8  9  10 11 12 13 14 15 16 17 18 19 20 21 22 23 24 25 26
M  A  R  S  U  C  V  F  W  G  X  L  Y  O  B  D  Q  H  E  T  Z  K  I  N  P  J
```

Page 17

Answer: BOGSTAR

Pages 28-29

Page 63

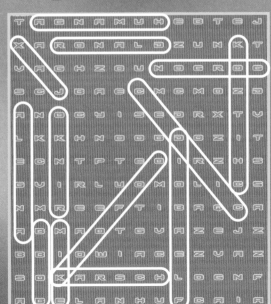

Pages 66-67
ANSWERS - TEST YOUR GAK

1. Klaktor
2. A chicken's egg
3. PCD
4. A disused missile silo in the Mojave Desert
5. No
6. Dark Comet
7. Erase his memory with a Memory Erase Pyramid
8. Do-Wah
9. They have hover capabilities
10. Laser staffs
11. They are wide open and glowing
12. Exo-skeleton
13. Dr Damage
14. One Martian Air Bike
15. Penkhan devised the Earth Shaker
16. Their noses to blow green energy bolts – super snot
17. Mike
18. If one gets hurt, the other feels it
19. He sent him to Earth in a Rover Pod
20. He smells awful

Page 79

DEAR STOAT MULDOON BY THE TIME YOU READ THIS, YOUR HOVERVAN WILL BE MILLIONS OF MILES AWAY. WE'VE TAKEN IT ON A LITTLE HOLIDAY TO A GALAXY NEAR YOU. HOPE YOU DON'T MIND.

YOUR FAVOURITE MARTIANS,

THE BUTT-UGLIES

THE HOVERBOARD PARK GAME

SEE PAGES 38 & 39

Cut out or copy the counter pieces on this page or use your own if you prefer) and place them on position 1 at the start of the game.